THE PERFORMANCE TRAP

And How The Gospel Sets Us Free

JEREMY MAHAFFEY

ISBN 979-8-88751-888-6 (paperback)
ISBN 979-8-88751-889-3 (digital)

Christian Faith Publishing
832 Park Avenue
Meadville, PA 16335
www.christianfaithpublishing.com

Printed in the United States of America

This book is dedicated to three people. First, a man named Brian Bishop. He was my friend from our first day of kindergarten until his death in 2021. The spiritual influence he had on my life is immeasurable, and the ministry I have today is accredited to his constant friendship. He was the first person to ever sit me down and clearly show me what God's grace truly was and how the performance of Jesus for me was more important than my performance for Him! Basically, He explained to me what grace truly was, and I am forever thankful for his influence in my life. But I am even more grateful that I was able to call him my friend for forty years!

Second, this book is dedicated to my mother, Brenda Mahaffey. She loved to write, journal, and send cards. When we were kids, if she was mad at us or had an argument with Dad, she would often write her feelings down, and sometimes it would be ten pages or more of her explaining her feelings to us. I really never gave much thought to those pages, letters, and cards in my childhood; but now I see the value of her taking the time to properly write out and explain herself. Therefore, I felt it only necessary to dedicate this book to her since she has written me many miniature books throughout my lifetime.

Third and last, this book is dedicated to the person who stole the original version that I wrote over ten years ago! Whoever this person is did not even know he stole it, but I hope whoever discovers it will be impacted by it. (I'll explain this more in the book.)

CONTENTS

INTRODUCTION

Everyone is a performer. Maybe not on stage or the big screen, but nonetheless, we all fight to control the narrative of our lives, and in doing so, we become performers. This book is my journey of being trapped by the feeling that my self-worth and value as a human was predicated upon how well I performed in all arenas of life. Regardless of whether it was Little League sports, my teenage years, or even the pastorate, I have often felt trapped by seeking my worth in my performance. The good news of the gospel of Jesus Christ is that you can have eternal life based on His performance for you and not your performance for Him! That is the entire basis of this book and something that I am eternally grateful for, and I hope to be able to explain this to you through these pages.

CHAPTER 1

The Beginning of the Performance Trap

Little League

I grew up playing sports: all sports. If it had a ball and a scoreboard, you could count me in. My earliest memories of life consisted of playing sports even before I can remember going to school. As a kid, I thought the four seasons had nothing to do with the tilt of the Earth in relation to the sun, but rather, they were the basis of which sport we were supposed to be playing. Summer was for baseball, fall was for football, and winter was for basketball.

I cannot remember a time in my childhood when I did not play sports. The thrill of victory and the agony of defeat were instilled in me shortly after Mom had weaned me off the bottle. There was one lesson that I quickly learned through my athletic childhood, and it was found in these two words: "Performance matters!" Winners were praised and star athletes were wanted, while uncoordinated kids that were slow and less gifted with a ball in their hands were regulated to the bench. As a young child, it did not take me very long to figure out that winning and losing were a huge deal, and my performance would always lead to one of those results.

One of my earliest memories was the desire to be the last batter in T-ball. In case you don't know what T-ball is, it's baseball without a pitcher for kids. The ball is placed on a tee, and the little sluggers hit it, and the rules are extremely lenient. The goal is for kids to learn how to play the sport at an age-appropriate level. The league that I played in allowed each team two or three innings depending on time, and every player was allowed to hit in each inning, making the last batter the most important. I quickly discovered that the coaches always wanted their best hitter to be last in the lineup in hopes of having runners on base in order to score as many runs as possible. I figured out that I wasn't the best player until I was the last batter. So as far back as I can remember, I was trying to perform in order to be rewarded. It's sad that I'm now in my forties, and I can still tell you the name of the guy who was the last batter on my first T-ball team, and it was my mission to be better than him. I can still see myself sitting on the bench, waiting my turn to bat while also realizing that I was not the best player. That feeling developed in me a competitive nature that is still in me today. As a five-year-old kid, I had already begun to understand that performance mattered.

Now I'm a couple of years older, my T-ball days are behind me, and my dad is coaching me in Little League basketball. He would always tell us in the pregame huddle that he didn't care what the scoreboard said; he only cared that we played with 100 percent effort. Even as a small child, I knew what my dad/coach was trying to do. He was preparing us for the fact that we might not win, therefore lessening the pain of defeat. But I noticed something as a seven-to-nine-year-old. Everyone in the stands really cared what the scoreboard said, and those with the most points always got the loudest praise. So for a brief few moments, it really did matter who "performed" the best. While my dad/coach was doing his best to help us kids have a good time, love the sport, and enjoy competition, I was noticing something different. Performance mattered.

As winners, we were treated differently. Even the conversations in the car ride home were different when we won. The adults in the stands spoke to us differently when we won. And on those dreaded nights that we lost, I can remember the strange way people really didn't have much to say. I noticed that the same people who were congratulatory to me in victory were very much absent and silent to me in defeat. The words and attitudes of those in the stands reaffirmed what I was already noticing. The better you perform, the more you are seemingly loved, praised, and wanted. The worse you perform, the less you are seemingly loved, praised, and wanted! It was the performance trap, and it had latched on to me at a very early age, and I could not escape it. But little did I know that everyone else was battling it too!

Tryouts

As a kid, I had signed up to play every sport I could through my local community center, and it wasn't until seventh grade that something seriously changed. No longer could you just sign up, pay for a jersey, go to practice, and play a sport. Now you had to actually try out and make the team. So now, performance truly mattered, or else you didn't get to play at all. It may not be a big deal to you, but that week of tryouts for my middle school basketball team was the most stressful week of my early life. It was also stressful because our small town did not yet have an actual middle school. Our elementary schools went through seventh grade, and our high school started at eighth grade. This made tryouts and stress amplified because the coaches could see and talk to the eighth graders all day, but we seventh graders really had no clue as to what was going on. Even when the team was picked and the cuts were finalized, the coaches would post the names on the door of the gym or the coaches' office. We seventh graders weren't at the high school, so we would find out the day of cuts to be made and then had to find a way to get to the high school and see if our name was placed on the sheet of paper posted on the doors. Remember, this was all prior to every human having a cell phone in their pocket.

I had analyzed my tryout performance down to the details. To this day, I still remember losing a speed drill where you had to score as many baskets as possible in a thirty-second time limit. Internally, I was in panic mode for finishing second place in this drill—never mind the fact that I had finished ahead of all the other kids except for one. I thought the coach was definitely going to cut me from the team. In my mind, why would he want the second-best kid? Remember, this "tryout" thing was all new to me, but I knew one thing was crystal clear. My performance really mattered.

When it was all said and done, I made the team! What a huge relief, or so I thought. Now I have to perform better than everyone else, or I won't actually get to play in the games. I thought if I made the team, then all would be right with the world. But all that did was relieve one stress and replace it with another. I'm on the team, but now I've got to perform well in order to get to play! As a seventh grader, I had already come to realize that the only thing in this world that matters is how you perform. It didn't matter if it was T-ball or Little League basketball. You must perform or else become a loser or, maybe even worse, you would become unwanted.

Maybe all this was just my competitive nature, or maybe it was all just part of growing up. But regardless, one thing was certain. The performance trap had me, and it would not let go. I literally became obsessed with sports because it was the one clear way that I could always gauge if I mattered. The scoreboard would always reveal whether or not I had value to this world. If I came up short, then I felt worthless. If I could score more points than you, then surely that meant I had real and substantial value, and that somehow made me feel like my life actually mattered.

Project Climb

When I was in elementary school in a small town in South Carolina, there was a program called Project Climb. In my class, there were three to five kids who always left school for about a half day or more and went somewhere else to learn something the rest of us didn't get to learn. As far as I could tell, this program took the smartest kids out of our classroom and rewarded them with some type of professional teaching.

I was obviously never chosen to be one of these elite kids. Every single time those kids left the room to go to Project Climb, all I knew was that they were being rewarded for being smarter than me. If I wanted to go, then I must academically perform better. I never did.

To this day, I still don't know exactly where those kids went, what they did, or whom they were with. All I knew was that they were performing better than me and, therefore, were receiving advanced training. The problem that I was facing was that in my mind, I had been tagged as not smart enough to go to this

Project Climb. And yet these kids were getting teaching that was going to make them even smarter than they already were. That meant I'd be falling even further behind, and it was frustrating me.

I can honestly remember thinking that I might not be better than these kids in the classroom, but I can promise you, I'm better than them at recess! It really didn't matter what realm of life you put me in. I was discovering that the only thing that truly mattered was how well you performed.

As an elementary school student, I was noticing that no matter what I did, I could not move beyond feeling that my existence as a kid was worthless if I did not outperform others in whatever arena of life I was in. The Project Climb kids were obviously smarter than me, and the teachers knew it, the other kids knew it, the principal knew it, my parents knew it, and I had come to the conclusion that everyone thought I was academically challenged. I felt worthless as a student, and my response turned into a hatred for school. I never rebelled against authority or caused my teachers any real problems beyond the typical kid stuff (that is highly debatable), but internally, I hated every classroom in that little three-hall-way elementary school.

Project Climb had become my performance trap that audibly said to everyone that I was of no academic value to the school. I didn't tell my parents, I didn't tell my friends, and I surely didn't tell my teachers. Instead, I just internalized my feelings that my academic performance was proof that I didn't really matter to the elite intellects of the world. In my underdeveloped brain, whoever ran this Project Climb program might as well have been the Secret Service of the United States government. To an elementary schoolkid, that's what it seemed like.

My performance in athletics had garnered me some self-worth, but now, my inabilities in the classroom had canceled that out. The performance trap had literally done just what the words said, and my young self had become its latest object of prey. There was no end for me in this feeling of my self-worth being dependent exclusively on my performance. And while the ball field had become my safe haven, the classroom had become the most painful place in the world for me. I could not find an end or even a healthy balance in this performance trap. If I hit a home run in baseball, that feeling of euphoria was quickly erased when the classroom laughed because I could not read and pronounce the word "island" in a book that I was forced to read aloud to the class. This may all seem trivial to you, but for me, this was the performance trap, and it seemed to have no end in sight.

Super Bowl Party

When I was a very small child, my family didn't go to church consistently. We had visited my grandparents' small Methodist church a few times, but in reality, church had no real influence in my earliest years. Then later in my childhood, my parents became Christians and started taking me and my two sisters to a Wesleyan church about five miles from where we lived. That church loved on my family, and my parents wouldn't trade those church people for anything. But for me, it was a very confusing experience. It wasn't that I was opposed to church, and the people at this Wesleyan church were extremely nice, but I just never could put all the pieces together. I would always wonder about some things:

- Where did the Bible come from?
- Why do I need to go to the front of the church to pray?
- Why are there so many other churches?
- Why doesn't anyone in the Bible have last names?
- Why do they check attendance? Doesn't God know who is there and who isn't?
- Why is the Lord's Supper so small?
- Why do you get promoted up in Sunday school but never have to pass a test?
- Why don't we know anything about Jesus as a teenager?

The list of questions could go on and on, but ultimately, church was confusing for me. I tried to suppress those feelings of confusion, but I never could get past the feeling that I was performing incorrectly. So, basically, my earliest memories of church consisted of being quiet and conforming to the people around me so that I wouldn't be rejected for poor performance. The reality of church for me was that I always felt like a confused outsider. At this Wesleyan church, I quickly realized that everyone else had already been there for years, and they knew things that I didn't, so I quickly felt like I didn't belong. There it was, the performance trap again. This time, I didn't know how to perform in order to belong to a church full of people who had been at this religion thing their whole lives (or so I thought). I was only a kid, but I already knew the way to get ahead and have significance in life was to simply perform the best. And even in church, this rule seemed to apply.

Fast-forward with me to my senior year of high school, and I'm only a couple of months from graduation. I'm at a Super Bowl party with pretty much all my high school friends. It was a party we had done every year since we were freshmen. But this year, things were different because the San Francisco 49ers were destroying the San Diego Chargers. So the game was a blowout, and everyone's attention turned to other things.

The owner of the house was talking with some of the guys about the end of the world. I was eavesdropping on their conversation because I wanted to hear what they were saying, but I was also afraid of what they were saying. I tried to play it cool and just listen, but the more I heard, the more terrified I became. Near the end of their conversation, Brian—one of my friends since kindergarten, whom I knew to be a Christian—was very confident in his approach to the subject. I vividly remember turning to him and saying, "Brian, I don't have inside of me what you have inside of you!" That's about as close as a teenage boy will get to saying, "Show me how to be become a Christian."

Brian knew me well enough to know what I meant. He immediately asked me to leave the party with him, and we went to his home, where he walked me through the gospel, the plan of salvation, Jesus's death on the cross, and what grace really is. For the first time in my life, someone said to me that my performance did not matter! I was excited and still a little scared, but I was glad to finally have what I thought was some closure to the performance trap.

I was overjoyed to know that my obedience was not going to keep me in God's good graces, and my future mistakes (which were sure to come) would not cause me to fall out of favor with God. *I was in awe that I could have eternal life based on the actions of someone else!* I was also a little bit mad that I had wasted my high school years trying to perform in order to be accepted by everyone, including God!

Just when I thought the performance trap would no longer hold me down, sure enough, it would rear its ugly head again. I had found peace and hope in my new relationship with Christ, but I was in agony trying to figure out how to balance being a Christian and also being accepted and approved by all the people who knew me prior to this conversion. I had no clue what I was in store for as a new follower of Christ. I thought the performance trap was tough through Little League and academics, but nothing prepared me for the vicious nature it would take in the church and with other Christians!

The Performance Trap and the Gospel

Definition and Performance

Let me define the performance trap for you. It's the internal feeling of self-worth depending on correct external actions. Now let me define it for you in Christian terms and in regard to the gospel. It's the internal feeling of salvation based on your outward religious activity. The opposite is also true; it's the internal feeling of being lost based on your external actions of disobedience. The problem is that outward actions and inward feelings become the basis of salvation instead of the work of Jesus Christ. The performance trap can be so deadly to our understanding of Christianity because we will base things on how we feel instead of on the truths of the gospel. Our feelings can shift like the wind. That's why we have to fully grasp that our performance is not the determining factor in Christianity.

It is true that outward actions should follow salvation and become the visible results of a person following Christ, but outward actions are not the cause or the keeper of salvation—Jesus is! In John's gospel account, Jesus said, "No one will snatch them out of my hand."[1] He didn't say, "Your obedience will keep you in My hand, and your disobedience will cause you to be removed from My hand." The beauty of the gospel is that God is glorified through the actions of His Son. He saves us based on what He did and not on how well we perform. So when it comes to defining the performance trap, I would argue that we must understand, articulate, and present to the world that their hope for salvation is found in the

---

[1] All scripture references are from the ESV (English Standard Version) 2005 copyright 2005 by Crossway. Wheaton, Illinois 60187.

outward works of Jesus's death on the cross and not on the outward works of the individual.

Let me be crystal clear. I fully believe and understand that a person should be obedient to the commands of Christ. My point is that our outward actions do not cause our salvation; they accompany it. Let me illustrate this for you. When I was a college student at Gardner-Webb University, I took a class that covered the sacraments of the Lord's Supper and baptism. We had thoroughly discussed the subjects and even wrote papers on them, and I will never forget asking the professor this question. "Professor, is it possible for a person to be baptized and take the Lord's Supper and still go to hell?"

The professor answered, "Yes!"

I then asked, "So that means it's also possible for a person not to be baptized and not participate in the Lord's Supper and yet could still go to heaven?"

The professor answered, "Yes!" And then the professor probed further by asking me a question. The professor said, "Jeremy, what conclusion can you draw from this?"

My response was simple. "No outward activity on my part can ultimately save me. Only the activity of Christ's death for me will suffice."

The professor responded with a spirited "You got it!"

It was truly a crossroads moment in my education, and it aided in eliminating the performance trap from my understanding of the gospel. Please don't think that I am advocating for Christians to ignore or abandon the sacraments of baptism and the Lord's Supper. Not at all. I'm arguing that these things do not cause salvation. They are merely acts of obedience that accompany it.

The performance trap can become so subtle and yet so damaging because if we aren't careful, then we'll see people performing, even in church, in certain ways. And we may automatically assume things that may not be true. The reason we are obedient to Christ in observing His sacraments is not so that we will be saved, but rather, we participate in them because we are saved. Far too many people see the outward activities of religion as having the power to save, but that's just the performance trap at its finest!

Jesus, Pharisees, and Performance

The ministry of Jesus, according to the Gospel accounts of the New Testament, goes directly against the performance trap. While on earth, we continually see Him rewarding those that didn't perform the best. The first time I actually read through the Bible, I started to notice this trend at work. Jesus rewarded those who trusted Him and not those who simply performed better than others. Jesus wasn't at the temple passing out perfect attendance awards, but rather, He was in the community looking for hurting people that He could help or even forgive.

For example, in John's gospel account in chapter 8, we are introduced to a woman caught in adultery. I think we would all agree that adultery is wrong, and in biblical times, it was cause enough to be stoned to death. The most religious people in the world brought this seemingly wicked and sinful woman to Jesus to receive her due punishment. Then by a flip of the script, Jesus doesn't punish her but shows her grace and then gives a stern warning to the religious Pharisees against casting stones.

This is just one of many examples where we see the ministry, message, and life of Jesus flying directly in the face of the performance trap. Those that deserve to be rewarded, Jesus warned, and those that deserved to be punished, Jesus forgave. The Pharisees were the most religious, law-abiding people on planet Earth, and yet Jesus said that "their hearts were far from Him."[2] Yet it was an adulterous woman that seemed to truly understand His grace. How is it that the most religious, best-performing, churchgoing, and commandment-keeping people were the very ones Jesus didn't reward? The reason is because Jesus was and is much more concerned with the condition of the heart than He is the performance of your religious duties. The Pharisees were trapped by their performance, and they couldn't possibly understand that a person could be saved while not doing all the things they were doing. Technically, their actions were all good things, but their hearts were missing the point. They had become addicted to the letter of the law above the spirit of the law.

---

[2] Matthew 15:8

The performance trap was not a backdrop to their life. It had become their life, and they set out to perform correctly at all costs.

Following the law was a good thing. Actually, in the Old Testament, it was required. But the Pharisees refused to offer any grace or forgiveness to anyone (unless, maybe, it was one of their own that had messed up). So performing correctly became far superior to the actual condition of their hearts. An evil heart that had correct outward conformity to the letter of the law was more acceptable to them than a forgiving, gracious heart that often failed.

This is one of the reasons the ministry of Jesus was so often rejected—because the Pharisees could not possibly imagine a Messiah who would come offering grace instead of rewarding their self-righteousness. Grace is a concept that nearly everyone loves, but one that most people truly struggle to accept. We want to have eternal life through Jesus and His death on the cross, but there is often a small piece of our soul that wants to say our efforts have earned us a right standing with God. We can all relate to the adulterous woman caught in sin, but the Pharisees hated the fact that Jesus seemed more intent to forgive her sin than to honor their performance.

Three Not-So-Little Words

The Bible records for us seven statements that Jesus made while He was being brutally executed on a Roman cross. Disclaimer: Everything Jesus said is important. But for this subject matter, I would argue that the following three words are the most important. Jesus said, "It is finished."[3]

What is finished? Was His life finished? Was Judaism finished? What exactly was finished? The work needed to provide salvation for mankind is now complete. His death was substitutionary and sacrificial, and therefore, those three words are critical for a proper understanding of the gospel. The death of Jesus on the cross was the work needed to provide us with salvation and to give us the forgiveness we needed. No amount of effort on my part is

---

[3] John 19:30 (ESV)

needed for salvation, and no amount of effort on my part will achieve salvation. That is why Jesus said, "It is finished."

The performance trap will make you change the quote from "It is finished" to "It is being worked on." As flawed humans, we desperately want to feel the accomplishment of having played a role in our salvation, but Jesus substituted Himself in our place and did the work that we couldn't do. Therefore, "It is finished" isn't just another verse in the Bible, but rather, it's the basis for you to be able to eliminate being trapped by the continual need to perform!

The performance trap is a double-edged sword. If you get it right, then you feel accepted, approved, and vindicated. You have worth and value. If you get it wrong, then you feel useless, unworthy, unwanted, and at best, damaged goods. This vicious thought pattern is in us without most of us even noticing it. Make the team and you have worth. Don't make the team and what are you? Make the grade and you are important. Don't make the grade and you're overlooked. Get the job and you have value. Don't get the job then who are you? The performance trap can and will destroy you. And while nothing will ever stop the gospel message of Jesus Christ, the performance trap can keep Christians paralyzed by the need to continually seek self-worth in their performance.

There have probably been plenty of times in your life that you have felt worth based solely on your performance, as well as plenty of times that you have felt useless based on your failures. What if I told you that 100 percent of your value, worth, and peace depended on the performance of someone else? Most people would panic at that thought, but the gospel of Jesus Christ is exactly that. We are redeemed, forgiven, and secured—all because of the performance of Jesus and not ourselves!

This is the double-edged sword that the performance trap will present you with. You'll want so badly to do something as an individual to be worthy of salvation that you'll continually battle the feeling of acceptance by God based on what you do. The opposite side of the sword is that you'll feel unworthy based on your wrongdoings. This is why the gospel is such beautifully good news: because salvation is given based on the work of Jesus and not on the work of the individual. So while the Bible may seem overwhelming, your life may feel overwhelming, and your career may be so time-consuming that it makes everything feel overwhelming, I plead with you to relax and find peace in this. Jesus did for you what you could not do for yourself. And when He did it, He proclaimed, "It is finished!"[4]

Listen to people share their testimonies in a church or in small groups, and I guarantee you that you will hear them say things like "Jesus saved me, and I quit doing drugs" or "I gave my life to Jesus, and I stopped drinking alcohol" or "I got saved, and I made all my wrong relationships right again." These testimonies are without a doubt true. And also, they are amazing because God saved the person. Each time I hear a testimony, I celebrate that God has redeemed a soul that was otherwise hopeless. But notice how subtly we just can't help ourselves when it comes to the performance trap. Jesus saved the people in the prior testimonies, but they had to

---

[4] John 19:30 (ESV)

also add something that they had done. Testimonies often become much like this. Jesus saved me, and look what I did? It's because even on our best day, we still want the gospel to be a little bit about what we've accomplished when it is really all about what Christ has accomplished for us!

A wise and humble gentleman who lives in my community once brought to light for me how the performance trap can be subtle and how it can be a poison to what Jesus actually did for us. He said, "Listen to people in the church talk. And if you listen carefully, you'll hear an underlying tone that talks about life in terms of sinfulness being a past-tense word."

His point was that we live our lives as Christians under two banners. One banner is the life before Jesus, back when we were sinners. And now the new banner is our life with Jesus and how we've somehow moved on from sin. News flash! You'll never get to a point in your life where you can say, "Back when I used to sin." This is why a complete understanding of the three words of Jesus is so critical:

"It is finished!"[5] The performance needed for us to be saved wasn't our own, but rather, it was the performance of Jesus on the cross. So our sins past, present, and future have been covered by His gracious act and not by our efforts through religious duties. Those three little yet powerful words of Jesus are what allow us to live with freedom and joy and without the need to continually try to measure our performance against anything from T-ball to the congregation of a church.

----

[5] John 19:30 (ESV)

The Performance Trap and the Church

Sunday School

I want to tell you about the first time I ever went to a Southern Baptist church Sunday-school class—or at least the first one I can remember. After becoming a Christian, all I did was go to my church's worship service, but over time, people kept inviting me to attend a Sunday-school class. I had been to Sunday school before at my parents' Wesleyan church, so I knew how this game was played. To be honest, I was not thrilled about attending a school that you could only graduate from by dying!

A few years after placing my faith in Jesus, I finally gave in to some of my friends and went to their Sunday-school class for college-aged students. I was terrified in this room even though I knew everyone there from our high school days. The teacher brought cinnamon rolls for the class to eat, so that quickly helped ease some of my fears about the class. Once the actual class time started and she began to teach the Bible, I was desperately hoping that she would not call on me to read, pray, or speak. I would really like to go unnoticed in this room of twelve to fifteen college students, which was basically impossible since I was the only new guy in this tiny square room.

Not long after the class started, I was feeling comfortable that this was going to be a lecture, and my fears of having to do or say anything were quickly alleviated. Then it all changed when she started asking questions. To this day, I still remember that for some random reason, she asked if anyone in the class knew what Romans 10:9 said. Everyone just sat there in silence for what seemed like ages. So, finally, after no one spoke up, I just blurted out, "If you confess with your mouth and believe in your heart that God raised Jesus from the dead, then you will be saved."

I can still, at this very moment, see the class turning to look at me. Then this one particularly loudmouthed girl turned to face me and said in front of everyone, "How did you know that?" Her tone led us all to believe that she (and probably the rest of the class) was shocked that the new guy knew something about the Bible that they didn't. I just couldn't help myself, so I responded to her by saying, "How could you not know that?"

Little did they know that for the past couple of years, I had been memorizing scripture on subject matter that I knew would be beneficial for my faith journey. One of those subjects was salvation, and Romans 10:9 just so happened to be in my memory bank. The problem I had was that before I went to this Sunday-school class, I had envisioned that they all knew everything about Christianity and the Bible, and therefore, I was the odd man out.

I left church that day discouraged because I thought to myself, *How could these people attend this church their entire life, and here I am, new to the game, and they don't know simple things like Romans 10:9?* For the record, I didn't attend that class much more after that day.

Allow me to show you how the performance trap works in the church. I thought everyone in this Sunday-school class had all the answers, and therefore, I felt inferior to attend. Then I attended and knew something they didn't, so instantly, I felt superior to them. The performance trap made me go from scared and inadequate to instant pride and arrogance. It seemed like everything I did caused me to seesaw back and forth between performing wrong and feeling inadequate to performing right and feeling prideful. When it came to church life, I just could not get a handle on this. I would succeed at something, and the performance trap would puff me up. I would fail at something, and the performance trap would beat me down. It seemed like an endless cycle in the church that I wrestled with. I was truly starting to understand why the apostle Paul said in Romans 7:15, "For I don't understand my own actions. For I do not do what I want, but I do the very thing I hate."[6]

If the writers of scripture battled this, then I was coming to the conclusion that I would have to as well. The bigger problem to me was that inside the church, no one prepared me for how to battle pride when I succeed and how to overcome defeat when I failed. That's not a stain against my church; they did everything they thought they were supposed to do. They invited me to Sunday school, they were kind to me, they shook my hand, and they talked to me. I even got to take up the offering on a few occasions, which helped me to feel like I might actually belong. The church did what they thought they were supposed to do; the problem was that they didn't actually help me learn how to deal with the feelings and attitudes that the performance trap brings.

My friend Brian had done a great job at explaining the gospel to me on the night of my salvation, but I wasn't prepared for the onslaught of spiritual battles I would have to fight through the perfor-

---

[6] Romans 7:15 (ESV)

mance trap. I had no clue about things like spiritual warfare, the armor of God, and petty church arguments. I was never angry at my church for not helping me with this internal performance battle. I had just come to the conclusion that I was going to have to figure it out on my own, and I'm still battling it to this day.

Now that I've served in the church for many years, I know why I didn't have help overcoming the performance trap. There are often too many needs and not enough willing workers to meet those needs. I didn't need food, water, or clothing. The Lord had blessed me with those things, and I have no doubt that if those had been my needs, the church would have met them. What I needed was spiritual help, and I needed some questions answered and some things clarified. I didn't know how to go about it in church apart from raising my hand, interrupting the preacher's sermon, and just flat out asking him out loud! I did not want to be rude, but I also did not want to ask things that might make me sound foolish. Yet again, the performance trap was at work in me even while trying to get honest help and answers.

The more I began to take my faith seriously, the more questions I had. The more questions I had, the more people seemed to avoid me. I could not seem to find a healthy, honest, and much older believer who would take on all my questions.

That was until a man named Rob showed up. My friend Brian had always been there for me during my faith journey. Even during times when I would go off the deep end, he would reel me back in. But it all changed when Rob came into the picture!

Our church had a fairly large group of eighteen-to twenty-two-year-old young adults who were too old for the traditional teenage youth setting but were too young to find a place with the aging adult congregation. Therefore, Rob took on teaching a class for that age group, and I attended from day 1. The reason Rob was so influential to me is because he was the first Christian to ever say these three words to me: "I don't know."

In one of our class meetings, we were discussing forgiveness, and Rob read Matthew 6:14–15, which I will paraphrase for you: "If you don't forgive others, God will not forgive you." I asked Rob in front of the class, "Does that mean that a person cannot be saved if they refuse to forgive others?" Rob answered me and said, "Based on these verses alone, I don't know!"

For the first time in my life, I was literally turning backflips on the inside, and I was elated not because Rob didn't know the answer, but because Rob was honest enough to say that he didn't know the answer. The irony is that I desperately wanted someone or a group of people to be able to answer all my questions, and yet it was the one guy who didn't have an answer for me that I grew to respect. I think that Wednesday night Bible study with Rob was the first time that I realized there were other people out there just like me—seeking, learning, and striving to know yet honest and transparent about their uncertainties or weaknesses. The church is a beautiful and glorious place of people with a myriad of problems and questions. The sooner we admit that we all struggle, the sooner we can all deal with what our real problems and questions are.

I have come to the conclusion that many sermons simply answer questions that people aren't really asking. I recently had a pastor of a small church in a rural community tell me that he was about to begin preaching a series on the dangers of anti-Calvinism. I asked him how many people in his congregation were struggling and dealing with this issue on a regular basis. He said, "I'm not sure, but I want to preach through it." I can answer that question for him: *none*! That's how many people in his congregation are waking up on a Monday morning and struggling with the dangers of anti-Calvinism.

When I was brand-new on my faith journey, I had many questions. Is it a sin to watch pornography? Will you go to hell for cursing? Is it a sin to drink alcohol? Is there a quota in the Bible that says how often I must go to church? My questions were honest and sincere, but it seemed like I had no avenue to get them answered. This is another reason I respected Rob so much. He seemed to be in this boat with me. He wasn't someone who would put up a religious smoke screen of jargon to cover up for lack of knowledge. I knew Rob's class would not last forever, so I was soaking up everything I could from those forty-five minutes each week.

About a year or so prior to Rob's class and just before my first Baptist Sunday-school experience, I had come up with a plan. And at the time, it was a perfect plan. At least, for me, it was. I bought a green folder, which was the only color the Eckerd store in my hometown had. It was the three-ring-binder kind, and I filled it with paper. Then at the top of each individual page, I wrote whatever subject I wanted answers for. I wrote things like "Cursing" on one page, "Alcohol" on the next, and then "Dating/ Marriage" on the next until I had listed all the subjects that mattered to me. I then started scouring through the Bible to find every single verse of scripture I could that directly addressed whatever subject or situation I had listed at the top of my pages. This was all before Google and the internet made these things readily available, and it was also long before I knew anything about systematic theology or hermeneutics.

So I read the Bible daily and often late into the night and started to find the answers to most of my questions, yet some of them still remained a mystery. Why am I telling you this? Well, I didn't have someone personally helping to show me the ropes of church life and to answer the questions of my faith. So my little green folder/notebook seemed as good a plan as any.

One more thing. Remember the girl from Sunday school who asked me how I knew what Romans 10:9 said? It was in my green folder under the subject heading of "Salvation"!

Saved by Attendance

Many local churches have been notoriously bad about drawing a direct line from outward activity to automatic salvation. I recently visited a very sick man in the hospital who was not a member of the church I pastored, but I knew him from my community, and I also knew the church he had been a lifelong member of. While visiting with him, I asked if he was a Christian and prepared to die. He said, "Yes!" What followed next was the sad reality of too many churches and Christians alike. He looked at me, called me by name, and said, "Jeremy, I have gone to church my entire life, and you are the first person to ever ask me if I am a Christian." He went on to say, "Everyone has just assumed that I'm a Christian because they see me at church each week, and they know I'm not involved in anything terrible, so they have all just decided I'm saved. But no one ever specifically asked me until you just did."

The performance trap can cause us to miss the true condition of the heart of a man because we become blinded only by what we see him do outwardly. My spirit was immediately crushed at the thought of a man attending church his entire life with no one ever asking him about his salvation or lack thereof. I'm sure the church never intentionally sought to ignore this man or overlook his true spiritual condition, but too many times, we are all guilty of assuming certain inward qualities based on outward or visible actions. Once again, it's the performance trap, and even the church body as a whole isn't exempt from it. To avoid this happening, we have to be strategic in helping people as well as specific in our conversations with them. We cannot and should not assume salvation just because they are in our buildings. Actually, the fact that they are in our buildings or attending our services ought to make our job of carrying out the Great Commission that much easier simply because we didn't even have to go find them. They came to us!

I have actually had people get offended, frustrated, and, on a few occasions, angry just because I asked them if they were Christians while we were at church. I've often wondered how it's possible that it could actually bother a person to have someone ask them if they are a follower of Christ unless, inwardly, they are not actually what they are outwardly. The tough role of the church—especially here in the Bible Belt of the Southern United States—is that we can assume salvation based on faithful attendance to a certain building when, in reality, we can't know for sure without asking.

So next Sunday at your local church service, go sit next to someone and ask them if they are a Christian and prepare yourself for a strange look or maybe even a snappy answer. But if that person smiles and answers with great joy, then stay close to that member!

Church Growth

I have been in some type of pastoral ministry for over twenty years, and without a doubt, the number 1 question I have received over two decades has been this: "How many people go to your church?" When I was a youth pastor, it was always "How many kids are in your ministry?" People who ask these questions do so with innocence and a true heart to know the answer, but in reality, it's the performance trap readily at work in their minds and hearts without them even knowing it. The real reason people ask that question is because they want to measure you up against their views of church or maybe even against their own congregations. The performance trap says that if your church is numerically large, then you are faithful and successful. The performance trap says if your church is numerically small, then somehow, you must not be a good or faithful preacher. The performance trap gets its claws in the numbers game of church life very quickly.

Think about this. Why do we never have a church conference that demands megachurches and their leaders to listen to faithful shepherds and God-ordained men who serve in small, difficult places where numeric growth may not ever happen? The answer is simple. We see large as better and small as a failure. This is the performance trap at its absolute best (or should I say worst). When it happens in the life of an individual, it says you are loved and saved because you have correct outward religious activity. When it happens in the life of a church, it says that you are to be applauded because your numbers are large, and you are to be shunned because your numbers are small.

Don't misunderstand me. I'm totally in favor of church growth and one million percent in favor of seeing as many people as possible come to faith in Jesus. The problem I have is that the performance trap will quickly conclude that the numerical size of your congregation is directly tied to your worth or value as a congregation, and the two things are not always correctly linked together.

The first pastor I worked under once told me something about church growth that I never forgot. He said, "Cancer grows, and it's not a good thing. Sometimes, to get healthy, you must first get smaller." His point was valid, and I think the performance trap is so deadly to congregations because many want numerical growth at any cost.

I'm learning more and more to value the wisdom of men who have faithfully served in difficult rural and struggling places. Once again, let me be clear. I'm not against large and in favor of small. I'm also not advocating that large church preachers are all sellouts. What I want you to see is that the performance trap can quickly make us think that large always means better, and small always means faulty, and that is not true. What is true is that there are gospel-centered, biblically based churches of all shapes and sizes, and we must not play the comparison game and allow the performance trap to derail the faithfulness found in small, medium, large, and even extra-large churches!

CHAPTER 4

The Performance Trap and Pride

The performance trap can give us an inflated view of self-worth. If we don't carefully monitor our thoughts, then we are susceptible to believing that we are what we do. The performance trap is so dangerous because if you start believing that you are what you do, then guess what happens when you make a mistake? You'll go from prideful certainty based on your right efforts to defeated self-loathing based on your wrong efforts. Then self-worth becomes a picture much like volatile Wall Street stock: up and down.

As Christians, we must constantly gauge how we value ourselves. If performance is the measure, then we'll constantly live entrapped by our own efforts rather than finding our significance and certainty in Christ alone. If you believe that God loves you more because you obey more and He loves you less because you fail, then your view of Christianity is flawed into your performance for God and not in what Jesus did for you.

Our attempts at salvation based on performance and not on Christ will ultimately lead to pride. If you're not extremely careful, you'll become a Pharisee without even knowing it. Pharisees were the religious elite, and although we know them to be extremely prideful and arrogant, their efforts to be obedient were to be commended. The problem with pharisaical living is that performance for God will often trump God's performance for you! There is nothing at all wrong with wanting to obey and perform correctly, but be careful that your obedience to God doesn't lead you into prideful arrogance. When you start down the slippery slope of trying to perform for God, then rest assured that pride will become your downfall. Correct performance will harass you into trying to achieve or hold on to your salvation by outward activity.

In his book *On Being a Servant of God*, Warren Wiersbe writes, "God is as concerned about the servant as He is the service. If all God wanted to do was get work done, He could send His angels, and they would do it better and faster."[7] I think his point is accurate that God's ultimate goal is to see our hearts changed through His grace based on the death of Jesus. Our attempts to earn God's favor will always fall flat or, even worse, make us prideful. One of the surest signs that you have begun down this path is that you'll start teaching and demanding that people become like you instead of pointing them to Christ. It's a dangerous game to play when we start demanding outward change and conformity to our ways rather than offering inward change through the gracious, forgiving, and loving act of Christ's death for us.

The performance trap can give us an inflated view of self-worth, and that feeling can be addic-

---

[7] Wiersbe, Warren W. *On Being a Servant of God* (Grand Rapids, Michigan: Baker Book House, 2007), p. 25.

tive. Go back to my seventh-grade basketball team. I somehow felt that I had more worth and value than the kids that didn't make the team. Some of the kids that "got cut" were my best friends, and for most of my childhood, we had played sports together. But now pride was creeping in. I was not more valuable because I could put a ball in a hoop, and they weren't lesser humans because they couldn't. But at that time, I could not and did not want to escape the feeling of superiority that I gained by making the team. The euphoria of success was addictive, and I wanted to do everything in my power to keep that feeling.

This is what the performance trap does. It wraps you up in yourself and your own feelings and consumes you. The good news of the gospel is that it frees you from this folly. You aren't superior to anyone. Those that made the team and those that didn't have equal worth to Christ!

Self-Hate and Performance

The performance trap also gives us the exact opposite feeling from inflated self-worth to deflated self-loathing. It can make us depressed, downtrodden, or even suicidal if, somehow, we can't perform well enough to gain approval from others or from God. The negative side of the performance trap is dangerous because we allow our downfalls to put us in a permanent state of sorrow. But, in reality, the death of Christ that gives us forgiveness should make us joyful, knowing that our mistakes aren't eternally held against us.

If you are reading this and you grew up going to church, then you've probably heard this statement from well-meaning people: "I'm just a poor ole sinner saved by grace." (I'm saying this in my best Southern dialect.) While this statement may be technically true, it also brings to light a reality inside the person as well as their potentially wrong view of God. This type of thinking is that, somehow, I perform so poorly that God's grace to me is just barely enough. And therefore, I'm just a poor ole sinner.

It's the subconscious thought that "God wouldn't really want me" and that "my performance has been so bad that I'm barely worth saving."

The performance trap can lead to a lifestyle of pity that makes the death of Christ seem feeble. As Christians, we are not just slightly saved. We didn't sneak in the back door of Christianity, but rather, God graciously and powerfully redeemed us from our sins through the finished work of Jesus Christ. This news should keep us from the opposite end of pride and allow us to live with the freedom of knowing God desires to have fellowship with us. You weren't his last choice in a long list of things he would have rather had, but the performance trap can make you believe that God would rather have someone else than you. When this thought pattern enters our minds, then defeat, depression, and self-loathing are sure to follow—none of which are the desires of Christ for you.

Back-and-Forth and Performance

Another major problem with the performance trap is that we all struggle to balance it. What I mean is that some days you get it right, and some days you don't. Sometimes your performance will be awesome, and sometimes you'll wonder how you could be so foolish. You'll have seasons of life where everything works out and seasons where it all seems to fall apart. During these times, our view of God shouldn't change just because outward situations do.

The performance trap can lead to pride, but it can also lead to depression. And it also has the ability to quickly shift between these two extremes. We have to come to grips with the fact that our performance can't be the permanent factor in how we feel about ourselves or in how we view God. We can't see God as good because our outward circumstances seem pleasurable, and we can't see God as bad because things don't go our way. If we only see God through the lenses of our situations, then we'll continually flip-flop between thinking "God loves me" and "God hates me" based on whatever we are facing at that moment. God is sovereign and gracious regardless of the hand we are dealt. When we come to faith in Jesus Christ, our mistakes no longer define us, our successes no longer puff us up, and we don't have to live constantly being tossed back and forth between these two extremes. We now rest in the assured hope found in Christ's death—not in our efforts.

I've had the wild swings or problem of the performance trap happen to me in a matter of hours. One committee meeting goes well and I walk out feeling valuable and thinking about how good God is. Then I enter into another meeting of irate church members who hate me and want to know why I made a mistake. I then instantly wonder why God is picking on me, and I struggle to figure out how I've failed Him. Do you see how our outward performance as well as our outward situations can quickly lead us astray from the truth about God? God isn't good just because you have a good day, and He isn't bad just because you have a bad day. But that is exactly what the performance trap would lead you to believe.

Let me give you an example of how things can quickly teeter between success equaling worth and failure equaling shame. This weekend, my wife and I were watching the NFL playoffs, and a professional kicker missed the game-winning field goal as time expired. The media was ripping him. The headlines were brutal, and I'm sure he was distraught. After the game, he said in an interview that he looked forward to going home to see his dog because he knew that his dog didn't care if he missed a kick!

Think about this kicker. He can literally do something that 99.9 percent of the world can't even come close to accomplishing, and he missed by mere inches. Now he feels like a total failure with no worth or value. This dude can kick a football better than most of us can do whatever jobs we do, yet the performance trap has him engulfed in feelings of worthlessness when it's simply not true. This guy would not be a better human or a better father, husband, or brother (if he is any of these things) just because the ball went three inches in one direction or the other.

The opposite side of this situation is also true. What if this NFL kicker had made the kick? Would his feelings of worthlessness be immediately replaced with an overwhelming sense of joy? I'm sure they would. But guess what? If he makes the kick now, the other team feels the way he does about missing the kick.

It's a never-ending cycle when we find our source of significance in our performance and not in the work of Jesus Christ's death for us. Allow me to clarify that I am not advocating for a lifestyle of being stoic, but rather, I'm vying for us to find our joy and hope in Christ and not in our performance or circumstances. I'm not saying the kicker should have run off the field smiling and happy because he missed, but he isn't any less valuable to God because he kicked a football three inches in the wrong direction. The performance trap can suck us all in, whether we are an NFL kicker or whatever profession we might be in. Therefore, we must continually hold tight to what Christ has done or else live a life that puts all our hopes and dreams in things like whether or not a football is kicked through the uprights!

As you can see, the performance trap can make you feel too lofty about yourself as well as too lowly, and it can even quickly switch between the two. The difficulty we often face in walking with Christ is that we take our worldly feelings of success and failure into our faith journey. The beauty of the gospel is that God's love for me is not based on my performance for Him. My whole life, everything has been about my performance. Make good grades and get more scholarship money. Follow the teachers' rules and you get ice cream. Do what the coach says and you'll get to play. Do what your parents say and you won't get disciplined.

It's nearly impossible in our culture to escape the performance trap. We all often make the mistake of believing or feeling that God loves us if we obey Him, and He hates us if we fail. This thought pattern has been ingrained in us through nearly everything, but the gospel of Jesus Christ follows a totally different route. I have value, worth, and forgiveness because of His actions and not mine.

No one is immune to the performance trap; even pastors battle it. I preach a good sermon and everyone leaves church telling me what a phenomenal delivery that was, and I instantly feel like I'm a person of worth. I botch a sermon, have poor illustrations, and my words come out confusing and everyone leaves rather quiet and reserved, and I instantly feel like a failure. There have been times when I have preached a terrible sermon, and I felt just like I did in seventh-grade basketball tryouts, thinking, *This church is going "to cut" me from being their preacher*. If your preacher is not exempt from the performance trap, then rest assured that it's coming for you too!

CHAPTER 5

The Performance Trap and Confusion

Not Even a Sermon

The performance trap has an uncanny way of creating lots of confusion. Many people sit in church their entire lives and wonder if they have done enough. I have seen this scenario play out a million times, where someone has an emotional experience or maybe they lose a loved one or have some huge life event drive them to a sudden and blazingly hot desire to live for God. They will attend church every time the doors are open, volunteer for everything, buy Christian T-shirts, and refuse to listen to anything that's not Christian on their car radio. They will download every megachurch pastor's podcast, and they will start, but not finish, reading all the latest Christian books (like this one). Then after a few months (and in some cases even weeks), that blazing hot desire for God starts to wane into frustration, and before long, they are right back where they started.

Why is this? Because they thought outward activity could earn them God's favor and give them the internal peace they so desperately desired. I'm not saying people should not do all these things. I'm saying all these things will not save you, keep you saved, or give you permanent peace. Only Christ will. These outward activities can surely be of value and be useful, and in most cases, they are acts of obedience to God. But these things cannot and will not save you.

I recently had a man that I respect say something to me that, at first, made me angry. But his explanation was spot-on. He said, "Jeremy, none of your sermons will ever save anyone." So after my initial shock and pushback, he elaborated by saying, "Your sermon will not save anyone. Only Christ will." We then talked for a while, and he spoke of a sermon as simply being the tool Christ may use. But the end result is that Christ—and not my sermon—is what saves a person.

It is true that the performance trap can consume even preachers and Christian teachers. We often struggle to separate our work from His work. Just like the laity that thinks doing more will earn them God's favor, the preacher often struggles to remember that it's still Christ and not the effective sermon that saves. The Bible even says, "It pleased God through the folly of what we preach to save those who believe."[8]

Obviously, we should be diligent and prepared in our preaching and presentations, but we must remember that our sermons are just tools to present to the masses the saving grace found only in the finished work of Jesus Christ.

---

[8] 1 Corinthians 1:21 (ESV)

Just Say It Louder

I vividly remember helping a church member move from one house to another, and his furniture and heavy appliances were to be loaded up in a huge moving truck. Myself, a couple of other church members, and three guys I did not know were there to help. These three other guys could not speak or understand a word of English; they only spoke and understood Spanish. An older gentleman from church who was helping found himself talking to these three guys, and they, of course, didn't understand him. So his response to them was to speak louder and louder until he was literally screaming at them.

I still remember laughing hysterically at this old man trying to talk to three guys who could not understand English, and he somehow thought, *If I just say it louder, they will get it.* Of course, they never did.

Many people feel this way about Christianity, and many ministers feel this way about their sermons. Just say it louder, and it will bring clarity.

That is not always true, and sometimes the world does not need you to scream at them. They need you to explain it to them or maybe even demonstrate it for them. In some cases, they just simply need you to walk with them through life and show them the gospel in every valley and on every mountaintop. Let me give you two examples of how confused the world (even Christians) can be about the gospel and our performance.

I recently asked a fifteen-year-old boy to define for me what exactly the gospel was. He said, "It's living for Jesus!" He was fairly confident in his answer although his voice was a little shaky (typical of any teenager talking to the preacher). This kid didn't know it, but the performance trap had already warped his thinking. He saw Christianity as his performance for God and not the other way around.

I was speaking once with a very seasoned youth minister, and we engaged in some serious theological discussions. I asked him if he believed it was possible for a man to have faith in Jesus Christ and yet still go to hell. He promptly replied, "Absolutely. If the man falls into sin!"

So, as usual, I pressed the issue and asked him to describe to me what he meant by "falling into sin." He said, "If a man falls into a life of sin, then it doesn't matter if he professes Jesus. He will ultimately go to hell."

I asked him if one sin would indicate that the man had fallen into sin, and he said no. So I asked him if one hundred sins would indicate that the man had fallen into sin, and he said yes. I asked him if sixty-one sins would indicate the man had fallen into sin. He said, "I'm not sure." I asked again if forty-nine sins would be enough. He said, "I see where you are going with this!" I told him his flaw was that his understanding of the gospel was based on what he does for Jesus and not on what Jesus did for him!

The performance trap is so deeply rooted in us that a random fifteen-year-old all the way to a seasoned youth minister can have it cloud their understanding of the gospel without even noticing it. These two guys both meant well. They spoke well, and they seemed pretty certain in what they believed. The problem was that both had a view of the gospel based on their performance rather than on Christ. It's easy to see pride on display in the life of an arrogant man. It can even be easy to see despair on someone's face when they've failed. The truly hard thing to notice is when the performance trap has someone confused. When we see the gospel through the lens of what Christ has done for us instead of what we do for Him, that is when confusion becomes clarity. I can't tell you the number of sermons I've heard, classes I've sat through, and conferences I've paid to attend only to leave even more confused.

It is my opinion that a good teacher takes a complicated subject and makes it simple, whereas a bad teacher takes a simple subject and makes it complicated. Jesus proved this point in Matthew's gospel account. The Pharisees were trying to trick him, and one of them (a lawyer) asked Jesus this question: "Teacher, which is the greatest commandment in the law?"[9]

Jesus responded not with a complicated answer but, rather, with a simple one. He said, "You shall

---

[9] Matthew 22:36 (ESV)

love the Lord your God with all your heart and with all your soul and with all your mind. This is the first and great commandment."[10] And to clarify the subject even more, Jesus said, "And a second is like it: You shall love your neighbor as yourself. On these two commandments hang all the law and the prophets."[11]

Jesus took the complicated question of the law and gave a clarifying and simple answer that didn't bring more confusion.

The performance trap is antithetical to the ministry and message of Jesus. He isn't looking for us to put on a show for Him much in the way the Pharisees were doing. He also doesn't desire that we live defeated lives because of our mistakes. The performance trap says that your outward actions should determine your feelings, but the message of Jesus simplifies everything. He substituted Himself for us and took on our sin, and now His desire is that we love Him supremely and we love our neighbor as

---

[10] Matthew 22:37–38 (ESV)
[11] Matthew 22:40 (ESV)

ourselves. It's Christ's love for us and His substitutionary death that gives clarity to our lives.

Confusion and Hypocrisy

Without a doubt, there are hypocrites in the church, but that doesn't make the church unique. There are plenty of hypocrites in all walks of life, but for some reason, the church is usually the only place that gets the blunt end of this claim. I've never heard an athlete quit a team and claim that there were too many hypocrites on his team. I've never heard someone say they are canceling their golf course membership because of all the hypocrites there that don't really love golf. I've never heard someone say they are going to quit shopping at Walmart or online from Amazon because those businesses are full of hypocrites. Yet when it comes to the local church, this idea of it being filled with hypocrites seems to be an all-too-common excuse used for people to stay away.

The performance trap is one of the main reasons the world so readily makes this claim against the church. We present ourselves as one thing on

Saturday night only to present ourselves as something else on Sunday morning. When this is true, then technically, the world is right, and we are hypocrites. The definition of a hypocrite is simply "one whose moral standards and their personal conduct do not align." It's as if they are performing. Does that sound familiar?

This is how the performance trap and the local church's reputation of being hypocritical can be so closely linked together. When we routinely perform in unchristian ways and we also routinely claim the title of Christian, then there is no wonder the world is confused over the message of the gospel. The real issue isn't that the world thinks we are hypocrites. The real issue is that when we are hypocrites, we don't own up to it and confess our faults and show the world God's grace. The performance trap and the hypocritical lifestyle will eventually end badly because neither the world nor the church will know who you really are.

As Christians, we must try to destroy this stereotype—not by just living with more outward religious activities but, rather, by living with more personal integrity. When a person comes to faith in Jesus, their life must begin the process of changing. I will be the first to confess that everything in my behavior was not instantaneously fixed on the night of my salvation. My soul had been redeemed, but my lifestyle, actions, and words were and still are a work in progress. Let me make sure you read this in the present tense. My lifestyle, actions, and words *are* a work in progress.

The performance trap will be so deadly to your maturation as a Christian because it will not let you release the way you had been living and accept the new life in Christ. It will cause you to be perpetually stuck in a state of flux between living a Christ-centered life and living a worldly life. When we can rest in the fact that Jesus has already performed correctly on our behalf, then we can have the confidence to live a life of transparency and integrity, and the confusion over the gospel and hypocrites will begin to fade away.

The Performance Trap and Culture

The Bible Belt

Here in the southern part of the United States, we are often referred to as the Bible Belt. Meaning that, basically, there is a church of some kind on every street corner. If you drive through the South, you will find this term to be very accurate. It's hard to go anywhere without the presence of some type of Christian denomination.

This influence and saturation with church life can actually work against the cause of Christ. Please hear me closely that I am not against the church at all, but rather, the familiarity with church lifestyle can actually work right into the hands of the performance trap. Generations upon generations have known the right things to say and the right way to present themselves around the church, its workings, and even its laborers.

For instance, I commonly hear people swear, curse, or gossip in my presence, only to then quickly turn around and apologize to me. Why is this? Because our Southern culture has ingrained in people that there is a certain standard of living associated with the church or, in my case, with the preacher. Why do people feel the need to apologize when I'm around? Simply put, it's the performance trap that undergirds their thinking.

Some may argue that we don't actually live in the Bible Belt anymore and that things are changing so rapidly that it is hard to even keep up with exactly what the culture is. As a student at Gardner-Webb University, I once had a professor ask our class for a show of hands as to how many students come from a broken home. Half the class raised their hands. The professor went on to explain that by the time we graduate, those of us from traditional home backgrounds would be in the minority. The incoming classes into the university would most likely and forever be made up of students not raised in a traditional home, where the child's biological father and mother were married and had raised the student. From now on, the culture would be vastly different from what most people in the Bible Belt had been used to.

The breakdown of marriage and homelife is not the only factor determining the culture we live in, but there are a myriad of things all contributing to a new type of normal. The performance trap is ready to engulf anyone in our culture regardless of his or her family or educational background. I remember that class at Gardner-Webb, and that day, I began to truly realize the world was changing, and I could not help but think how this would impact the church and how we think we must perform.

The gospel of Jesus is an unchanging message, and the church must do its best to clearly promote that message through faithful, loving, and devout followers. We also must pay attention to the ever-changing culture around us.

Recently, I had a close friend being interviewed by a church to become their pastor. He told me that one of the questions the committee asked him was whether or not he would preach using a leather bond-paper Bible or an iPad. He went on to say that they were harshly against anything electronic in the pulpit and even went so far as to say, "If it is electronic, then it's not the Bible!" This is a blatant disregard for the culture we live in.

Now I know that many of you are going to be quick to jump on the fact that Christians are not supposed to conform to the culture, but rather, we are to be different from the world. I totally agree, but at the same time, we must be able to engage with the people in our communities and in the world around us. And while our message is always the same, the package in which we deliver it may be different today than it was in yesteryear.

The performance trap is so dangerous when it comes to the culture in which we live because it will always have us trying to measure up to some imaginary standard of living. I used to think that everyone was watching my every move and that, as a preacher,

I truly lived in a glass house. But the longer I serve in ministry, the more I am noticing something else at play. Most people are not concerned about me at all because we are all too wrapped up in ourselves to be concerned about people we barely know. The old saying is that we are all trying to keep up with the Joneses, but in reality, this culture is not trying to keep up with the Joneses. We are trying to surpass them!

This is where the performance trap will once again come into play. As a Christian, the enemy will tell you that you do not measure up to certain people in your church or community. Therefore, the culture will force you to put on a performance that makes everyone appear that they have it all together all the time!

I think one of the greatest impacts you can have on your culture is not success but transparency. Our culture has trained us to be positive and upbeat at church or the grocery store or the local sporting event. As Christians, we do not often live in a world of total honesty nearly as much as we live in a world of cover-up. Not in the terms of some grand conspiracy or some massive illegal operation (although that is possible), but we have learned to be so superficial and shallow that the performance trap leaves us consistently putting on a show and has caused our culture to lack transparency.

Think about this. How many times have you run into someone at church or in public and asked the simple question "How are you doing?" Inevitably, the response is always the same. "I'm fine. And you?" Everyone cannot be fine all the time, can they? Surely someone somewhere had a bad day or is going through a hard time, but the performance trap has us locked in on covering up our flaws so the culture will not see us as failures.

I am not advocating that we all live in a world where we just dump out our dirty laundry on everyone at every occasion, but I am saying that the performance trap has us in a perpetual state of shallowness and maybe even phoniness so that we don't seem like failures. As Christians, we must live in such a way that we feel no need to be fake because our worth is not predicated on how other people perceive us but, rather, on what Christ has done for us.

Social-less Media

You would have to be living under a rock to believe that social media has not impacted our culture more than anything since the invention of the internet. My eight-year-old nephew and my eighty-year-old aunt both use social media in some capacity.

It is extremely difficult to find someone who is not at all impacted by the use of social media. The church I pastor has people posting and sharing my sermon quotes even before I make it home for Sunday lunch. The positive side of the social media's impact is that information can spread quickly, whereas the negative side is the same fact. Oftentimes, wrongful, hurtful, and slanderous information can also spread quicker than you could ever imagine.

How does Facebook, Instagram, and Twitter play a role in the performance trap of Christians and churches? Most people who engage in social media only allow themselves to be viewed in a certain context. While users rarely see it as performing when they use social media outlets, the truth is that we can easily become enamored with how many likes we have or how many people share our posts. Many will spend hours trying to get the perfect picture to portray a certain lifestyle, and these just add fuel to the fire of social media addiction.

Last Christmas, my wife and I went to Punta Cana. It was the first time in my life that I was not at home for Christmas. That year, my mom had died from cancer, and my friend Brian had also died from cancer. The man who was the chairman of the deacons at my church and had become a dear friend also died, and my wife's aunt passed away. All these happened within a matter of weeks. To say the least, it had been a brutal year. So my wife and I, along with her sister, decided this was the year to just get away for the holidays.

While we were enjoying Christmas morning on the beautiful beaches of the Dominican Republic, I couldn't help but notice the countless young ladies taking pictures on the beach. Taking pictures on the beach is nothing new, but these girls weren't just taking a picture. They were taking hundreds (if not thousands) of pictures, and they were also taking hours to review them so they could post the perfect ones on whatever social media app they were using.

This is what the performance trap does to us. It forces us to try to control the narrative of our life and make sure that people only see us in our best picture. The performance trap will cause you to use social media to promote yourself and not Christ. I know lots of ministers who post videos, devotionals, and sermon clips ad nauseam. I cannot help but wonder if this is done out of a desire for the church to be edified or if we are addicted to the feedback and possibly even to the sound of our own voices. We must remember, as Christians, that our performance is not the determining factor in salvation, but rather, it is what Christ has done for us. Therefore, we must guard against using social media to promote ourselves even if it is under the disguise of a Christian message.

The performance trap will be sneaky when it comes to social media because it may present itself as harmless and lighthearted fun, but the reality is that you may actually be using it to find your self-worth and validation. This sneaky tool of the enemy has caused many people to actually become less social by using social media. It brings an addiction to the *ding* of a new like or the number of reacts to a post. When this starts happening, then people are not actually engaging with people but, rather, devices. Please hear me clearly on this. I am not anti-social media. I use it and try to engage with it but also keep in perspective what is happening with others who are involved with it.

A couple of years ago, I decided to take some extended time away from all social media, and I found out that it became increasingly more and more difficult to even have a conversation with people because every interaction began with someone saying, "Did you see this on Facebook?" or "Have you seen that Instagram post from someone?" I literally was struggling to talk to people in my own church family simply because I had disengaged from social media. It has impacted our culture in ways that we have never seen before.

The performance trap is also deeply ingrained in the fabric of social media. Watch what happens when someone finds out they have been tagged in a picture they do not like. You can literally watch them have a meltdown. Why? Because we want to control the narrative and perform in a certain way, even on cell phone screens!

The danger we all face with social media is not that we use it too much but, rather, that we replace our need for Christ with our need for "likes." Our culture may be rapidly changing with the instantaneous nature of information being shared with and through social media platforms and the continual self-promotion that it leads to, but let us not forget that our salvation, self-worth, value, and forgiveness are not found in a hashtag or a repost but, rather, in Christ alone!

CHAPTER 7

The Performance Trap and Family

The Breakdown

I spent the first ten years of my ministry working with teenagers, and I was consistently battling the broken home dynamic. Kids growing up being tossed between parents' and family members' homes has become the norm for our society.

I will never forget this one particular kid who told me that he hated Christmas. I was, of course, floored by the statement and pressed him as to why. I knew he had come from a broken home and that his homelife (or lack thereof) had impacted his underlying behavioral issues. He told me that he hated

Christmas because he had to go to all of his families' homes, but I was still confused as to why this was such a problem. He went on to say that he had to go to seven different homes on Christmas Day in order to be a part of all the divorces that have made up his family. I thought he was exaggerating, but he was telling the truth. I, on the other hand, came from a traditional home setting, and therefore, I could not comprehend his situation. And yet it was normal for him.

Situations like this one are now all too common, and a new generation has grown up without truly knowing where or what home is. The breakdown of a homelife where the father and mother raise a child together from conception to adulthood has almost become a thing of nonexistence, and the performance trap has been right there the whole time, seeking to devour. Kids learn to perform one way at Dad's to garner his love and, possibly, another way at Mom's to earn her love. And this game spills over into every other area of life. Mom becomes afraid that the kids will want Dad instead of her, so she caves to the pressure of the kids, and the same is true for Dad. All the while, the kid is learning to play the game of performing to earn love and value. The problem is that it becomes difficult for a generation to understand the gospel of Jesus Christ's love for them and how it is not based on their performance but His!

Along with the kid who had to attend seven homes for Christmas, I will also never forget one particular parent of a kid under my ministry. The mother wrote me a letter (I will refrain from using names) and stated in these exact words: "My son's lack of spiritual development is a direct reflection of your lack of leadership in his life!"

I will never forget that line as long as I live. I immediately set up a time to meet with this family, and the young man was utterly embarrassed. He told me repeatedly that his mother's statements were not true and that he had (in his words) "no beef" with me. Why did this mom write me this letter, and what was the real issue at play here? The more and more I dove into this situation, the more I realized that the mom desperately wanted the son and father to have a relationship that just wasn't happening. So instead of owning it, she blamed me!

This is why the performance trap and the home are so intertwined. The mom could not possibly tell the dad that he was not raising his son right. The dad was too insecure to even try to parent an aggressive teenage boy. So the performance trap in that home went something like this. Mom learned to walk on eggshells to prevent Dad from getting angry. Dad learned to avoid his son under the banner of manhood being equal to silence. Son learned to perform by just doing whatever made him feel good at the moment.

I am sure, if you are reading this, that you have witnessed many scenarios just like this one or at least very similar. The performance trap will cause a home to cave to the pressures of cultural stereotypes instead of gospel-centeredness. I do not pretend to have all the answers on fixing what ails our society and broken homes, but I do know that I have witnessed hundreds (if not thousands) of homes where the performance of Christ on their behalf has taken a back seat to personal performance for individual success, pleasure, and the desire for love.

While I am writing this book, I just attended an elementary school fifth-grade graduation where they gave all thirty-eight kids an award! Do you know why they did this? Because the performance trap has taken over our society, and we are terrified to tell someone they are not good at something for fear of social media backlash. Newsflash: Your kid needs to learn that they aren't always the best.

I can still remember the first time I played Little League football, and at the end of the year, we did not have a team banquet. We had a league banquet. They gave out awards for the best offensive player, the best defensive player, and the overall league MVP. There were probably a hundred kids or more in that banquet hall, and only three kids left with a trophy. I can still remember thinking, *If I want to play sports, I am going to have to improve a lot and work harder to become as good as those guys.*

In today's society, that would never happen because the league would be contacted by numerous parents complaining because their kid deserved an award too. The performance trap not only impacts kids but also parents alike. Kids want to perform to earn their parents' love, and parents want to perform to earn their peers' approval, and this vicious cycle never ends. But the gospel of Jesus is the only thing that can help end our incessant need for approval and validation from people.

If Mom and Dad are consumed with the performance trap and are always looking around and comparing themselves with other families, then one should fully expect that kids and teens will follow their parents' lead. I've heard many political pundits and wealthy media figures bemoan the fact that the breakdown or breakup of the home is the root cause of all that ails this nation or any nation. I would like to take it slightly deeper and add that the breakup of the traditional home is not an isolated problem, but it may actually stem from the selfishness that the performance trap leads to.

I've counseled with countless couples on the verge of divorce or already on the other side of divorce who claim that their reason for ending the marriage was that they just weren't happy. Once again, the performance trap rears its ugly head and makes couples believe that the performance of another spouse will finally lead them to ultimate happiness.

The irony of this folly is that happiness, not the gospel, becomes the means for which an individual seeks inward validation. Too many homes fall apart because of the performance trap. Kids believe parents will only love and approve of them based on grades, behavior, and/or athletic performance. And when those things suffer, then don't be surprised when Mom and Dad struggle to figure out what's wrong with the kid's attitude, self-esteem, and motivation.

When Mom and Dad clearly make the gospel of Jesus the defining fact of purpose and acceptance, then homes can withstand even the most brutal of storms. But if performing at a certain standard is the goal, then no one should be shocked when this imaginary goal isn't met.

CHAPTER 8

The Performance Trap and Possessions

Shoe Fetish

When I was a kid and teenager, I had a serious shoe fetish. I could not stand to have old sneakers on my feet. It wasn't that I had to have just new kicks, but it had to be "the" newest kicks! There's a slight chance that I haven't fully outgrown this fetish yet, but oh well.

My shoe fetish was so bad that I can still remember the Nikes I wore on my first day of high school. I can remember walking the halls of my high school or even the campus of my college and looking at and judging people on their shoe game. I know it's silly, foolish, and immature; but like I said, I had a shoe fetish, and it had me.

Actually, it was the performance trap yet again. I believed being able to afford the latest Nikes, Jordans, or (back in the early nineties) Reebok Pumps was a sign that I was performing better than others. I know it's wrong and it shouldn't be that way, but growing up, I always judged people on their shoes.

You may laugh at my shoe fetish, and you may think it's ridiculous, but you probably have something just as similar in your life. You may be struggling to make a car payment that is out of your league just to show the world you are performing better than them. You may be deciding between getting behind on your mortgage or getting behind on your power bill simply because you took on more than you could handle because you wanted others to see how well you are performing economically. There's an age-old adage that says, "It's all right to have stuff as long as stuff doesn't have you." I think that adage is spot-on. Many never overcome the belief that more stuff or newer stuff will ultimately result in happiness. It is a game that some folks play and never win.

In my first ministry position, I was the part-time youth pastor at Orchard Street Baptist Church in a little South Carolina town called Mayo. On my last Sunday serving there, the pastor and his wife had me over for lunch after the service. Once we finished eating, we were all sitting on their front porch, and the pastor's wife (her name was Liz) said to me, "Jeremy, I would like to give you two thoughts of advice before you leave us."

I was listening, but of course, I had heard all this kind of talk before. She is going to tell me to seek God and love God with all my heart. She is going to tell me how I'm going to do great things for the kingdom of God. All the normal stuff Christians in church work would normally say.

But I was badly mistaken, and her words still ring in my head more than twenty years later! Her two pieces of advice went like this. First, she said, "Jeremy, no matter what church you go to, they will all have the same problems, just different faces.

Second, if you can put a price tag on it, it will not make you happy!"

I was caught off guard by her bluntness as well as the randomness of those two pieces of advice, but little did I know then how correct she was. The performance trap will make you strive for material possessions as the ultimate goal for your happiness.

I still remember buying my first car and thinking that all my problems had been solved. I had worked and saved my money for three summers and paid $2,500 cash for a 1987 Honda. I thought all was right with the world. Then I quickly found out that I couldn't quit my little part-time job because now I needed money for insurance, gas, taxes, new tires, and of course, a better radio and speakers. Once again, the performance trap and the belief that materialism would bring me happiness only led me to more misery.

Let me be clear in saying that there is absolutely nothing wrong with having nice things, nor is there anything wrong with striving to have nice things. The opposite is true as well. There is nothing inherently godly about poverty. Sometimes the church immediately equates poverty with godliness and riches with sinfulness, but that's not always true. But what is always true is that the performance trap can quickly grab hold of you in the realm of material possessions. I'll be the first to admit that I love that new car smell, and I love the feel of new shoes on my feet. I (like you) must fight for those things not to be the source of my ultimate joy; otherwise, my joy will flee quickly when the miles pile up on the car and creases get worse in my new shoes!

I remember once asking my mom why my neighbor gets more Christmas presents than I do. Mom quickly came up with some rationale about how I get more throughout the year than he does, and the other kid's parents must save all year for him to have one good day. I don't know if that was true or if that was just my mom's quick answer to appease me as a child. Regardless, there was one thing that was true. I saw his gifts and my gifts and immediately concluded that he was performing better than me.

So the performance trap has now impacted me in the classroom, on the ball field, and at church.

And now, even Christmas was a gauge for performance. This performance trap has consumed most of my life, and looking back, I struggle to find any area where it doesn't get at least a small foothold into the depths of my soul.

If you're honest with yourself, then you probably struggle the same way I do. We all have to fight hard to let go of materialism and cling to Christ and allow Him—not Nikes or Reeboks—to become our fetish.

The Performance Trap and Its Only Cure

The One Cure

My mother had a very unique battle with cancer. When she was twenty-nine, she was diagnosed with colon cancer. The doctors performed surgery and gave her a colostomy and said that all was well. Then in her late fifties, she started having some back pain and found out that the surgery from nearly thirty years prior did not ultimately clear out all the cancer. The cancerous cells had just been floating around in her body for years, looking for a place to grow. They finally settled on the inside of her pelvic bone, hence the cause of her back pain.

Not long after the discovery, my mom had multiple surgeries and more radiation and chemotherapy than any human should ever have to endure. The radiation and chemotherapy never did cure the cancer, only kept it at bay until, ultimately, Mom's frail body and compromised immune system just couldn't fight it anymore. The doctors in Spartanburg, South Carolina, and Chapel Hill, North Carolina, were awesome and did all they could, but there was no one magic pill that the doctors could find to cure her disease.

Until her dying day, my mom held tightly to the words of Isaiah 41:10, "Fear not, for I am with you; be not dismayed, for I am your God; I will strengthen you, I will help you, I will uphold you with my righteous right hand."[12] It wasn't until cancer came along for a second time that my mom truly understood that she could not "perform" for God's acceptance, but rather, He was the one holding her

---

[12] Isaiah 41:10 (ESV)

all along. The destruction the performance trap will leave in its wake is the belief that somehow, we can perform well enough or long enough to earn God's favor. *There is nothing you can do to make God love you any more or any less than He already does.* My mom learned this truth through a very deep and dark painful valley.

The performance trap can fade into the background of your life once you come to the realization that Jesus has already done for you what you could not do for yourself. Too many people believe that it wasn't enough for Jesus to save them by His grace, but now they think it's up to their performance to keep themselves saved. *If Jesus isn't strong enough to keep you saved, then He was never strong enough to get you saved!*

The destructive nature of the performance trap is that if you aren't careful, it will run roughshod throughout any and all areas of your life. My mom discovered that sometimes it took a dreaded disease just to realize that God's love was never dependent on her performance. Every area of her life was impacted by cancer, but the interesting part was that it took cancer for her to see that her performance wasn't what God was seeking, but rather, it was simply her heart.

I had the honor of giving my mother's eulogy, and one of the things I said was that my mom had become known as the woman with cancer, the dreaded "C" word. I reminded the audience that it was a different "C" word that truly defined her, and that word was "Christ!"

If you are not careful, the performance trap can define you, and it's a nonstop moving target that ends in frustration. It's a lifelong battle to overcome the feelings that our performance before the world is what gives us our worth, peace, and value. The great news of the gospel message is that it's not our performance that defines us any longer, but rather, it's what Christ did for us that can become the foundational truth on which our life stands.

The performance trap will impact your entire life if not quickly conquered. It has the power to control your marriage, your job, your kids, your hobbies, and most destructively, it can even derail your faith. That is why it is critical that Christians allow Christ to define them and seek to humbly follow Him instead of the ever-changing and broken world we live in.

Book Thief

More than ten years ago, I began writing this book. I had completed the first six to seven chapters, and here is where things get interesting. I was serving on the pastoral staff at a local church, and we had all our computers linked to a network. This was done for a myriad of reasons, some of which were calendaring, accountability, and just overall protection of the staff. One of the main reasons this was done was to back up and save all our work to the network (now that would be a cloud). I did not want anyone seeing this file or reading this book, so I saved it to my computer without linking it to the network so that the other pastors and secretaries could not read it. Then I did something very foolish. I did not save my work to any other external device, thumb drive, and the like.

During my writing of this book, the church office was broken into, and the thief stole my computer. None of the other guys were too upset because, surely, they knew I had everything backed up on the network. Well, I did have it all saved—everything except this book! I fully expect that the thief probably pawned our computers for a few easy dollars or maybe even sold them to another more honorable thief (sarcasm mine).

That church break-in felt like I had been punched in the gut by Mike Tyson. All my hard work for nothing, all that typing and retyping gone forever, all my experiences and soul-exposing thoughts simply gone without a trace. I keep hoping that someday I will get a phone call from a total stranger saying they bought a used computer from a yard sale or pawnshop and found a book on the desktop and took the time to read it and found that Christ was all they needed. I know this is beyond a long shot, and I don't fully expect that call to ever come; but if it does, you better believe that will be the sermon I preach that week!

Here I am almost fifteen years removed from my computer being stolen, and what does any of that have to do with my concept of the performance trap? Hear me out. I felt so proud of my work and was excited to see it in print. With the conclusion of each chapter, I was feeling more and more prideful at what I had accomplished. The moment it was stolen, I immediately threw in the towel and concluded that I was not meant to be an author and that my words were of no value. I was literally writing a book on the performance trap while fighting the feelings of how well I was or wasn't performing in writing it.

The performance trap is vicious, and as long as we're alive, it will be with us. To avoid its pitfalls, we must seek our peace and validation through the performance of Christ on the cross and trust what He has done for us as opposed to the continual need to feel like we must perform to be approved by God Himself!

In Conclusion

While I am writing this book, a man walks into my office to tell me that he applied for a new job, and he hopes his performance at the interview will be good enough to vault him to the top of the candidates. I sincerely hope he gets the job, and I hope he thrives in the new role. But more than that, I hope that he doesn't seek his ultimate joy in this position because one day, it will be gone. The performance trap was written all over his face, and he didn't even know it.

That is why I wrote this book. People all over the world have no clue they are current sufferers of this trap. It is a silent and almost undetectable disease that we all have, and rarely, if ever, do we discover it. It will grab you and not let go. It will control you at home, school, work, vacation, ball field—there is no place that we can go to that it isn't waiting to attack us again and again.

The only cure for it is actually a strange one. When a doctor finds out something is wrong with a patient, he either gives them medicine or schedules a surgery. But never does the doctor say, "I'll do surgery on myself, and it will cure you!" But that is exactly what happed with Jesus! The problem we had was that we were trying to perform in order to gain His love and eternal life, but we kept failing over and over. So instead of prescribing us a medicine, He took the medicine for us! Now it's up to us to trust Him because the cure isn't found in us but, rather, in Him!

The concluding point I would like to drive home is twofold. First is that everyone I know and everyone that you know is struggling with the performance trap. The second is that the only way to overcome the performance trap is to understand that you are defined by what Christ did for you and not in what you do for Him! No one is immune to feeling like their performance defines them or that they need to perform in certain ways to garner God's love. All Christians struggle with this. When you are at church, it's easy to see others and believe the lie that they've got it all figured out. It's easy to go to your local high school football game and feel the need to look and act a certain way to be accepted and approved of by the general public. This type of thinking gets into our heads, and eventually, it can hijack our faith and make us believe that God will only love us if we look, act, talk, dress, and appear a certain way.

Did you notice that all those things are outward issues? God is much more concerned with who you are inwardly far above what you appear to be outwardly. The inward man can change the outward man, but the outward man cannot truly change the inward man. This is the paradox of the performance trap. We believe that certain conformity to outward things will lead us to having inward peace, confidence, and hope. But it never does. The only thing that ever truly changes us and sets us free from the never-ending trap of needing to perform is when we fully trust Jesus because He said, *"It is finished."*

ABOUT THE AUTHOR

Jeremy grew up in the traditional small-town culture of Chesnee, South Carolina. He is the son of Bruce and late Brenda Mahaffey. The middle child, he has two sisters, Carole and Leslie. From an early age, sports and a love for fishing and hunting dominated his life, and they still rank at the top of things he loves. That upbringing and his competitive nature were the foundational issues that led him to write this book. Jeremy has served in vocational ministry for twenty-three years and is a graduate of Gardner-Webb University with a degree in religious education. He and his wife, Beverly, currently reside in Vale, North Carolina, where he serves as the senior pastor of Mount Vernon Baptist Church.